OUR GUIDE

OUR GUIDE

BY

FRANCIS X. LEVY

With a Foreword by
Father Charles Carpenter, M.A.P.

SECOND EDITION

Copyright © 2001 Francis X. Levy
Printed in the United States of America

ISBN: 978-1-62550-536-1

J
M
J

TO MARION AND MARY

IN HONOR

OF

THE BLESSED MOTHER

AUTHOR'S NOTE

This book was written in response to a request made by Father Charles Carpenter, M.A.P., the first Superior General of the Missionaries of Perpetual Adoration. It is my privilege to comply with his request. Original Publication was made in April 1985 on a very limited basis. The revised edition provides chronology, additional information and amendment of text.

In conformance with the decree of Pope Urban VIII, I submit the material in this publication for human consideration only. The Catholic Church unreservedly is the judge of extraordinary gifts of grace.

ARCHDIOCESE OF LOS ANGELES
1531 WEST NINTH STREET
LOS ANGELES, CALIFORNIA 90015-1194
(213) 251-3200

21 January 1986

Mr. Francis Levy
7124 Hellman Avenue
Alta Loma, California 91701

Dear Francis:

    Thank you for sharing with me a copy of your book "Our Guide" in which you relate some very special incidents in the life of Father Aloysius Ellacuria, C.M.F..

    I had great admiration and devotion for him and so I certainly encourage you to make your publication more widespread.

    The last time I saw him before he died he said to me "I will be able to help you more from heaven than I have on earth." Only God knows how many graces I have received through his intercession.

    May God continue to bless you and nourish you in your faith.

Sincerely yours in Christ,

+ Juan Arzube
Auxiliary Bishop of Los Angeles

aa

CONTENTS

FOREWORD

INTRODUCTION 1

TRAGEDY 6

THE PAINFUL JOURNEY 9

THE ANGELS 15

EXTRAORDINARY EVENTS 19

DIVINE CONSOLATION 43

ETERNAL REWARD 67

PERSONAL DATA 71

FOREWORD

"I never deserved any of the graces God gave me," Father Aloysius once explained. "However, when God gave me _any_ grace, even small favors, I thanked Him with all my heart. And whenever I thanked Him, He gave me more graces. So I am convinced that if we are grateful to the Almighty God He will give us many, many graces."

Herein lies precisely the merit of the writing you have in your hands: a grateful heart celebrates his blessings received. Gratitude has made the writer keenly aware of things that somehow we often pass over in our own lives. These are the beautiful gifts that God is giving us constantly, even more so in our daily crosses. The fact that some of the things the writer expresses are of a miraculous nature does not diminish what we owe to God in gratitude for the other more "hidden" graces. After giving alms, if the beggar smiles and thanks you, isn't it true that you feel urged on to give him something more? Similarly, our gratitude for little things is often what triggers in God this liberality or "holy madness" (I Cor. 1:25a), to give us further signs of His love, sometimes even of an overwhelming radiance. These latter kinds of graces seemed countless in the life of Father Aloysius.

Now, regarding the form in which this work is written: Now-a-days one of the channels through which the gift of faith is communicated by God to souls is what are called "personal testimonies" or witnessings. In a testimony one shares with others the marvels that Almighty God has worked, purely by His Infinite Mercy, in one's life (cfr. Mary's Magnificat, Lk. 1:46-55). In a sense, the Gospels too embody this form of writing. Through it, faith is awakened, stimulated and driven along in its growth. We all have something to gain by hearing these testimonies because we need to know how to thank God in His second causes. Regarding these second causes, Blessed Elizabeth of the Trinity (Nov. 9th), raised a few months ago to the altars, said, "There are no second causes." That was her way of expressing her gratitude. She saw God in everything, no matter how small or contingent it was.

Francis Xavier Levy lives in Alta Loma, California, where I had the privilege of being introduced to him and his loving wife, by Father Aloysius ten years ago. Many of us would like to be able to express in the same way Francis Xavier does our own gratitude to God for so many favors received through Father Aloysius. As Saint Teresa of Jesus says, "We would wish to have the tongues of angels and of men to praise Him."

Fortunately, God can read our hearts.

>Fr. Charles Carpenter, Sup. Genl.
>Missionaries of Perpetual Adoration

19 March 1985

INTRODUCTION

Throughout my life I have been singularly blessed by having holy priests in close association. It was the Oblates of Mary Immaculate who served in my home parish in New Orleans and administered the primary school that I attended. Hard working Irish and American priests were exemplary workers in the vineyard. During high school and college, I was trained by the Jesuits and had some excellent cleric and lay educators. In later years, I relied particularly on the Fathers of the Sacred Hearts. It was while in their midst that I was confronted with the tragic and spiritually awakening era of my life. Most recently, however, I became attached to the Claretians.

It is obvious to me now, that the Lord knew from the very beginning that I would need the best of help in order to guide me; so He never hesitated to provide. In times of greatest need, I could always be sure that God would hear my prayers. A vivid example was in 1950, in Bremerton, Washington during the Korean War (which had been the reason for my recall to naval service). I was assigned to a ship which was still in "moth balls" and was being re-activated for service. It was hardly habitable; therefore, portions of the crew including myself were permitted to live ashore. Realizing that I might never come back from this war alive, I seized the opportunity to have my wife, Marion, travel from New Orleans with me on this assignment to share a few weeks together. Our only child was left at home in the care of our parents, and Marion was in the latter stages of pregnancy with our second child. The weather was dismal, rainy and depressing; our quarters were in a simple motel along the road outside of town. In our last few days before I was sent with this ship overseas, while it was still being renovated, I left Marion one Sunday morning and obtained a ride with someone to the navy base for a day of duty as Officer of the Deck. I told Marion that if she wanted to go to church, she would have to hitch hike for we had no car. That she did, willingly, even with her physical discomfort. As a means of remaining together spiritually, we had swapped Rosaries -- my wooden beads had become hers and her large crystal beads with the ornate silver crucifix had become mine. Having boarded the ship to begin my duty, I dismissed the two enlisted men who were on watch at the gangway. I figured it was a good time for them to go below for coffee. Soon thereafter, I entered the officer's restroom and closed the door. Immediately, I noticed that the knob and shaft were missing, and the door was hopelessly locked. Realizing that no one else was on this entire deck, I knew that shouting or noise making would be fruitless; prayer alone would free me. Thus, I spoke briefly but confidently in prayer to Our Lady: "Dear Blessed Mother, if you want me to remain locked in this room, I will accept your will and wait until tomorrow when many people come aboard, and then surely, I will be found; or,

Blessed Mother, if you see fit, please let me out, so that I may go about my duties." I said one Hail Mary. Then, noticing only barren bulkheads, devoid of any implements, I reached into my pocket and found Marion's rosary. The ornate crucifix was the exact size to fit diagonally into the door latch, I turned it easily and opened the door.

Why, then, if Our Blessed Lady heard me so readily on this and other occasions, would she not hasten to help me later in life when I was in dire need. Surely, as a truly solicitous Mother she would send Father Aloysius, a most holy son of hers, to guide me. Yes, he would be my spiritual advisor for twenty years and share with me the sad and the joyful events that were to transpire. Countless others too would experience the effects of an encounter with this mystic priest. He would see Victor and Irma Duenas, Marion's parents, celebrate their 50th wedding anniversary with his blessing. Albert and Henrietta Levy, my parents, were also to be the fortunate recipients of Father's blessing.

Father Aloysius Ellacuria, C.M.F., a pious and humble Spanish missionary, a holy man of God, became my "Spiritual Father," and he filled me with joy when he called me his "Spiritual Son."

TRAGEDY

During November of 1960, it was on the tenth of the month, as I recall, my wife, Marion, had a biopsy performed at Pomona Valley Hospital in Pomona, California. Our sixth child, Ann, had been born a year earlier, exactly ten years after her oldest brother, Frank, thus completing a three time repeat of the boy - girl cycle. And it was in Ann that we had a brunette to go along with blonde Linda and the red haired Gail. We had a beautiful family for which I was thankful, but what was going to happen to it now? California had been our new home for only five years. At last, after years of struggling, the opportunity had come for professional advancement and the easing of financial pressure.

After hours of surgery, I was confronted by Drs. Naujokaitis and Crowley who came to announce their terrible findings. I was alone in the hospital as they spoke to me, and it was dreadfully alone and abandoned that I felt.

Yes, the lump in the breast was malignant, and a simple mastectomy had been performed. The prognosis was not good, only time would tell.

I was angry, very angry, and I didn't hesitate to let the Lord know how wrong He had been. Yet I prayed to Him just in case He wanted to change His mind. I went to our pastor, Father James Keefe, SS.CC., and begged for his prayers. My parents, brothers and sisters, always devoted and prayerful, never neglected me or mine in their heavenly solicitations. The Daughters of Charity of Saint Vincent de Paul (three of my sisters are in this order) and the Oblates of Mary Immaculate, who have a priest brother of mine, prayed for us as did many other religious and lay groups.

Neither radiation therapy nor the subsequent oophorectomy were able to stem the spread of cancer, but during this period we were blessed by a continuous series of events.

Priorities suddenly had changed. No longer were those demands of yesterday even to be remembered. I was now seized by apprehension and fear.

THE PAINFUL JOURNEY

During her convalescence from her initial surgery in November 1960, while I was at work one day, Marion was visited by a priest from Spain whose name I do not know. He was brought to our house by a woman, whose name also I do not know. She lived in Our Lady of Talpa parish in Los Angeles, where my eldest sister, a nun, had been stationed a few years earlier. This priest was anxious to spread devotion to Saint Anthony Mary Claret, the founder of the Claretian Order. The prayer which he left with Marion was a common leaflet, apparently printed in Spain. The net result of this visit was that Marion added this leaflet to her group of daily prayers, and we both disregarded the incident as nothing more than pious solicitude on the part of our visitors. Several weeks later, however, the woman wrote to Marion saying that she would be glad to introduce her to Father Aloysius. Since we had never heard of this priest (the superior at the

Claretian Provincial House in Los Angeles), and since we had our own parish priests nearby, I tended to politely dismiss this opportunity. Coincidentally, Mary Greene's daughter, Maureen, had recently stopped by with a holy article from Fr. Aloysius, and also, on the very same day that the letter came, Marion received a call from Mary Greene, who recommended that we attend Fr. Aloysius' novena on Sundays in Los Angeles. Mrs. Greene also stated that if we needed a ride, Dr. Herbert Morrow's wife, Katherine, would be glad to take us.

At this point, it seemed that everybody was impressed by Father Aloysius except me.

Out of curiosity, I took Marion to the novena in the old structure that was the Claretian Provincial House at 1119 Westchester Place. The novena was to be held in a very small chapel off of the main parlor at about 2 o'clock. The place was packed; the crowd overflowed from the chapel to the area outside of the doorway, a library, and over into the parlor. It was in this parlor that Marion and I were standing when Father Aloysius came down the steps. On numerous occasions in future years, he was to recount this first visual contact with me, even though I was unknown to him and surely he was unknown to me.

Father proceeded with the novena to the Blessed Mother and prayed to Saint Anthony Claret. After the service, he blessed us individually by placing his hands on our heads. Marion spoke quietly to him, telling him that she had cancer, and he said that he would like us to come see him during the week. I was working in Pomona at the time, and I thought it would be difficult to get time off to visit Father, but it turned out to be surprisingly easy. However, we never would have gone without an invitation. In fact, this first private visit was the beginning of many weekday visits (about on the average of twice a week), each visit being with his earnest invitation.

During our first visit, Father took Marion and me into the chapel where we prayed.

Father was using his Rosary, and I was greatly impressed by his devotion as he clutched his beads. In fact, I was so impressed that I silently hoped to have his Rosary for my very own. Shortly after we left the chapel, Father spoke to us and said as he turned to Marion: "I want you to have the Rosary that I used." With that, he presented his Rosary to her. In amazement I turned to Father and said: "My prayer was answered even better than I had hoped; I wanted the Rosary for myself, but you gave it to my wife."

The Rosary which Father had given to Marion was a specially indulgenced one which had been given to him. He had very few of them, but he left the room for several moments and soon returned with one for me as well. Father was very interested in these particular Rosaries since they had a special Indulgence applicable to the souls in Purgatory. Because of his interest in these Rosaries, I left not a stone unturned investigating a means of supplying him. Thus did he receive many.

Marion cherished her special Rosary, and at her death I saw to it that she was buried with it.

On each visit, Father's blessings were long and intense. Most of the time, I experienced an overwhelming spiritual sensation during his blessing. It was as though the Lord Himself were present. Almost always, a distinct fragrant aroma surrounded Father. On one occasion I went into the chapel to pray and noticed that Father Aloysius was also kneeling in prayer. He concluded his prayers, and I was left alone in the chapel. In a few moments I was distracted by the characteristic aroma, which I immediately attributed to flowers apparently in the garden outside. By looking completely around the chapel, however, I learned that there were no windows open, and there were no flowers inside either. Why, then, the aroma? Soon, it dawned on me that even though Father had left, his aroma lingered for several minutes. It was this fragrance that I had erroneously attributed to flowers.

Although we prayed hard, and Father blessed us frequently at his Sunday novenas and numerous weekday visits, Marion's condition grew steadily worse. In total desperation, I prayed privately one night: "Lord, what would You have me do?" A few days later, when we were visiting Father, he was explaining to us the splendor of the Angels and what their mission is. Marion and I were seated, and Father's eyes were directed at her. Suddenly, in the midst of his explanation, he turned to me and said: "God would have you do no more than you are doing." Dumbfounded, I addressed Father and said: "Do you realize that you have answered my prayer exactly as I said it?" Father smiled and cast his eyes downward, as he would usually do in humility.

THE ANGELS

Father was very devoted to the Angels and taught us to say the Angelic Chaplet. Through the years, we learned that:

The Angels are composed of nine Choirs--the Seraphim (whom Father often described as being a pure flame), Cherubim, Thrones, Dominations, Virtues, Powers, Principalities, Archangels, and Angels. The duties of these Choirs are: The Seraphim are given to the love of God; they are pure love and occupy the highest position among the Choirs. The Cherubim exemplify knowledge, and they stand next in rank below the Seraphim, Father also mentioned that some people have Seraphim and even St. Michael, too, as Guardian Angels. It seems that he meant these special Angels as additional to the regularly assigned Guardian Angels. The third Choir, the Thrones, are noted for submission to God's will and for peace. Thus, the first three Choirs constitute the First Hierarchy which is related to divine mysteries.

The Second Hierarchy, the next three Choirs, deal with the management of human affairs as follows: Dominations display zeal for the maintenance of God's authority. Virtues carry the message of the Dominations, and Powers fight against the evil spirits.

The Third Hierarchy, the final three Choirs, have these duties: The Principalities announce divine things. They are responsible for the protection of our country and of the world. They help every soul to attain the degree of holiness to which God calls it. Father also said that each church has an Angel from this Choir assigned as its protector. The Archangels are entrusted with the more important missions of men: the Pope, the Bishops, etc. Finally, the Angels, the ninth Choir, are messengers sent to men. Guardian Angels and special assistants to us are in this Choir.

Whenever Father spoke of the Seraphim and tried to describe them, he would begin as though he were going to give a detailed account of their appearance. Immediately, however, as he spoke, it became obvious that he must have seen Seraphs. He was hardly able to describe their beauty, except to say that they were pure flame, burning with love for God. From subsequent conversations I became convinced that he had them in his presence.

I learned too, that every home has an Angel assigned to guard it. Father said that we should have special devotion to the Angels (all nine Choirs), and that the Archangels, as we call Saint Michael, Saint Gabriel and Saint Raphael, may actually be Seraphim. He said that he knew someone who had St. Michael for an Angel. He explained in his talks that the word "Angel" as we use it, applies to all members of the nine Choirs and also happens to be the specific name of the ninth Choir. In like manner, we sometimes use the word "Archangel" to mean someone higher than an Angel, and it also is the specific name of the eighth Choir.

Father said that St. Vincent Ferrer is the sixth Angel of the Apocalypse. He also emphasized the devotion which St. Anthony Claret had for the angels and cited the occasions on which the saint was visibly assisted by them. In further discussion we learned that Our Lord had revealed to St. Anthony Claret that He had made him the seventh Angel of the Apocalypse. This latter fact was also published several years later by Father Aloysius in an article entitled: "Seventh Angel of the Apocalypse" which he wrote for the January-February 1971 issue of Soul Magazine.

EXTRAORDINARY EVENTS

The trips from La Verne to Los Angeles, made for many weeks, were beset by mechanical difficulties with our car. Seldom could we use the freeways for fear of breakdowns. Ultimately, I got wise and asked Father to bless our car. It was then that travel became much easier. When he gave us this blessing, he also blessed our children with Holy Water, and they thoroughly enjoyed it. At the age of three, Dan thought that this was wonderful. He and the rest of the children had such a beautiful love for Father that they would fall to their knees whenever he approached.

It would be impossible for Marion and me to visit privately with Father had the children not been provided for. Here also, was the hand of God upon us, for He had sent Joan Davis, a recent graduate from Mission High School in San Gabriel, to be our "daughter." Joan had been our babysitter at the Los Angeles Orphanage whenever we went there to visit Sister

Henrietta (my sister Gertrude); so she had become part of the family. At the time that Joan came to live with us, we didn't know how necessary her help would be during the painful journey that was to ensue.

In February 1961, Marion and I decided to become daily communicants during Lent, which was soon to begin. Marion, however, suggested that we not wait for Lent, but rather that we begin immediately on February 12th. Thus we began daily Communion and continued to follow this practice throughout Lent and beyond. When Marion became too ill to attend Mass, I would ask one of our parish priests to bring Holy Communion to her at home. At times, I felt that this request was too much of an imposition on our priests; therefore, I resorted to asking them frequently, rather than daily. Fortunately, however, I myself was able to continue to receive uninterruptedly.

On Sundays, we went to the Claretian House at about 12:30 for the 2 P.M. novena. There were a few seats on the veranda, which hardly accommodated the line that formed, waiting for the doors to open. We knew that space within the chapel was at a premium, and it was only by an early arrival that one could be assured of getting inside. When all of the seats on the veranda were occupied then those who arrived later would stand in line. We usually scheduled our trip in time for Marion to get a seat because she was quite ill, and for her to stand for any period of time was very tiring. One Sunday, while she was seated, waiting for the doors to open, she noticed that a woman, whom she deemed to be sicker than herself, happened to be standing. Feeling compassion, Marion gave her seat and position in line to her. Subsequently, when we went inside, we were in a poor location and in the middle of a crowd near the chapel doorway. When Father Aloysius had completed the novena prayers and was ready to impart his individual blessing on the congregation, he suddenly walked through the crowd and went to Marion to bless her first. It was as though he had seen the sacrifice that she had made and didn't want her to wait any longer.

Many sick people attended these novenas. Numerous physical and mental problems existed in our midst. Some of these people would be cured, but all, if they were in proper disposition, received miracles of grace. In his talks to the people, Father often informed the crowd of miraculous healings that Almighty God had effected in the preceding week.

First Friday was always a special day at the Provincial House. Several Claretian Guilds met during the month at Holy Mass, but I believe that the First Friday meeting was the most populous. Before the new house was built, it was necessary to use the chapel at the rear of the grounds, adjacent to the tennis courts. The additional space in this location, although not adequate, could better accommodate the crowd, and the rustic decor provided a peaceful setting.

Frequently, Father asked me to serve his Mass on First Friday. To attend the Holy

Sacrifice is surely our greatest privilege. Additionally, it is a special honor to be invited to serve. On one of these Fridays, after Father had finished the Mass and was about to begin Benediction, he ascended the altar, and then motioned back to me to indicate that he didn't have a monstrance. Right away, I left the altar and went into the sacristy. As I was walking, however, I felt within myself that the trip was futile; I clearly recalled that before Mass one of the Claretians had closed the doors to the cabinet that housed the sacred vessels. I had definitely seen him lock them before he left, heading for the main house. Nevertheless, I knew that I should at least try to open the cabinet to get the monstrance, because there was the possibility that he didn't do a good job in locking it. After all, Father was waiting at this time on the altar to begin Benediction, and he needed an ostensorium. How correct I was in my anticipation; my efforts to open the doors were fruitless. They were really locked! Disappointed and helpless, I went to the entrance of the sacristy, where I could see Brother Salvatore Azzarello at the organ. My motions caught his attention. He stopped playing and came past the altar into the sacristy to see what I wanted. When Brother heard my plight, he walked over to the cabinet and opened the door with ease. There could be no doubt then, that Our Lord wanted us to have Benediction that day.

During the same time frame, perhaps a few weeks later, another event relating to Benediction occurred. Father had exposed the Blessed Sacrament and was now kneeling at the foot of the altar reciting numerous prayers. I knelt by his side with the smoking thurible close at hand. It seemed to smoke excessively during these long prayers, and it was certainly getting hot. Then came the time for Father to offer incense. We both stood as I gave him the incense boat and kept the thurible. When I held it, I was surprised to see that is was not the conventional censer with which I was familiar. It did not have the usual two-chain system, one for support and one for operating the lid. Instead, this unit had a single chain which was attached to the base; in order to place incense on the burning coal, you would have to grasp the top of the chamber with your hand. I remembered that it had been smoking a lot, and by now the top could be very hot -- but then again, maybe it wouldn't be too bad. I held the base of the thurible in my left hand while using my right hand to grab the top. It was exceedingly hot! I had no choice but to drop the lid immediately. Father was standing there waiting -- incense boat in hand. The congregation was waiting, and most importantly, the Blessed Sacrament was waiting. There I stood, with two fingers on my right hand smarting terribly from the momentary contact with the hot lid of the censer. Promptly, I said a silent prayer before the Holy Eucharist: "Lord, I have two more fingers on my left hand; I'll give those to you, and then that's all I have." By changing hands, so that the base of the unit was now in my right hand, my left was free for a second attempt at the lid. Quickly, I grasped the menacing cover. I was able to <u>hold</u> it and lift it open with absolute comfort! Slowly and methodically, Father spooned the beads of incense over the glowing coals. Astonished, I realized that my left hand was immune to the severe heat. All this time, my right hand burned intensely. Later, in the sacristy, when services were over, Father said: "You burned your hand," as he grasped it with his own and rubbed my painful fingers. Immediately, the pain began to subside until it was quickly gone. I turned to Father and asked: "Why is it that these fingers on my right hand burn so badly after holding the top just for an instant, whereas, my left hand, which held the lid for so long, has no pain whatsoever?" Father's reply was: "God wants to show you how much He loves you."

There was a time when Father heard confessions on Thursdays at the San Gabriel Mission. On one such Thursday, June 1, 1961, Marion and I arrived at the Provincial House at about four o'clock. This was an unusually late time for us to visit with Father. When we did see him, he blessed us and apologized for not having more time to talk. He was in a hurry, because it was now about 4:35, and he was due to leave for San Gabriel. When Father left the room and I had the opportunity to talk to his driver, Brother Larry, I asked him if he knew how bad the traffic would be at five o'clock, passing through Los Angeles on the way to San Gabriel. Oh yes, he was quite familiar with it, because he drove Father that way every week at this time, but he surely didn't observe any traffic. Repeatedly, he stated that he never noticed any traffic. That, I couldn't understand, because everybody knows the traffic congestion in the heart of Los Angeles at five o'clock. In a few minutes, Marion and I drove off and took the route homeward right through downtown Los Angeles. As expected, traffic was following its usual heavy pattern. When we stopped for a signal light on Main Street, there on our left was the Claretian car with Brother

Larry and Father Aloysius. Father motioned to me to follow him, which I did. We then proceeded to drive all the way to San Gabriel as Brother Larry had predicted, without a traffic problem. It was necessary for us to stop only once during that trip.

When we reached San Gabriel, Marion wasn't feeling well. I got out of the car alone and went over to Father's car. He was delighted that we had come, and now he felt that he had the time to spend a few moments with me. I hadn't told him previously, but I needed to talk to him that day. How disappointed I was at the Claretian House when he told me that he wouldn't have time to visit. Now, in San Gabriel, the time was being given to me. God, of course, knew my needs and provided. I spoke to Father about the particular matter that concerned me. I was very thankful indeed for this opportunity. After that, Father and I walked through the garden. We went to the section that had been made into a small Claretian cemetery. It was here that Father told me he too wished to be buried. Providentially, his wish was granted. Twenty years later, he was laid to rest in this beautiful garden and Our Gracious Lord ordained that I would have the privilege of serving as his pallbearer.

One afternoon, we had a visit scheduled with Marion's physician, Dr. Lawrence Crowley. We had arranged also to squeeze in some time with Fr. Aloysius in the latter part of the morning. When we met Father, it was apparent that he was quite busy and didn't have his usual tranquility. After a brief chat, he blessed us and sadly announced that he had to leave. We tried to ease his chagrin, caused by the limited time that was available and mentioned that we must leave anyway for our doctor's appointment. At that, Father responded: "The doctor will say that you are better." Shortly thereafter, we left and proceeded to the doctor's office in Pomona. After checking in at the desk, we took seats in the waiting room with numerous other patients. Scarcely did I have time to pick up a magazine, when the door opened and the doctor come into the waiting room. He strode over to Marion, addressing her as follows: "Well, you're better." After this terse statement, without uttering another word, he dashed back into his office. In amazement, I sat there pondering the fact that this man, whom Father had never met, had just spoken the phrase which had been foretold.

Because of the great discomfort that Marion experienced with her illness, it was often difficult for her to sleep. In order for me to get adequate rest before going to work, I frequently slept in another room. About four o'clock one morning, I was startled by an overpowering sensation that I was not alone; rather, Father was there with me, putting me at peace. When I had the opportunity, I questioned him as to whether he had bilocated at that time. He answered with his usual downward glance and smile that he was not aware of it, but that other people had also told him of similar experiences.

In La Verne a towering ash tree gives mute testimony to the efficacy of a blessing by this holy priest. Our son, Steve, brought home a very small tree one day from school, a typical project for a youngster. We planted the tree in our backyard, but it didn't fare too well. That is, it didn't do well until Father blessed it on one of his visits. Thereafter, this tree flourished; the massive trunk always reminded us of its benefactor.

Father Aloysius was most diligent in his prayers, yet, he strove to reach greater heights. When I told him that St. Anthony Claret prayed very much, he took it as providential that he too must pray more.

Marion's education was provided by the public school system in New Orleans. Thus, she was not privileged as I was to have formal Catholic training. At opportune moments we discussed various aspects of our faith upon which I could elaborate. I remembered one case where these discussions prompted me to make up a story to illustrate a point pertinent to our topic. In the days which followed, I heard this very story repeated to us by Father Aloysius as a means of explaining his thoughts.

It is important to mention that whenever Father was granted an answer to his prayers, whereby a miracle or gift of any kind was received, he forcefully made it known, time and time again, that he himself had done nothing! Everything came from the Almighty God. Rarely did he use the word "God" by itself. He always preferred to say "Almighty God." His prayerfulness knew no bounds. He was not one for idle chatter, but he enthusiastically engaged in meaningful conversations and imparted earnest priestly blessings whenever the opportunity presented itself. Father often told us that every blessing provided grace. He went on further to say that sometimes physical healing occurred, but always, with proper disposition, spiritual healing was received.

In an effort to stop the spread of her cancer, Marion received radiation treatments. Her physical condition was very poor due to the deteriorated condition of her spine and the weakness brought on by radiation. It was at this time, and under these conditions in early 1961, that we made frequent daytime visits to the Provincial House to receive Father's blessing and spiritual counsel. On some of these trips Marion had to lie on the back seat of the car because she felt so badly. Then, upon arrival at the Claretian House, she required considerable help to negotiate the front steps. In the parlor, Father would bless her, and he would unfailingly follow up with the entreaty: "Now, walk down those steps." The steps referred to at this time were those at the back of the house, which were equally as steep as the ones in the front. Yet she traversed them with ease. She did not walk, <u>she</u> <u>ran</u>, up and down, over and over again, with no difficulty whatsoever. Fearful that she might hurt herself, I was always the one to bring this exercise to a close. Upon leaving the Provincial House, however, it was a different story. Marion would again return to her former condition of helplessness. At home she required assistance to go from her bed to the bathroom; a series of chairs would provide the necessary support. One day, our five year old redhead, Gail, saw her struggle. She stood firmly by the bed with her back toward her mother and said: "Mommy, you can lean on me." In the years that followed, I frequently reminded Gail of the tender love that she had given to her mother. She had not failed to notice the devotion often displayed by her nine year old sister, Linda.

By such frequent contact, Father came to know our children well. He had such an affectionate regard for Frank that he envisioned a possible Claretian vocation for him.

Marion had numbness creep up her arm, then envelop her tongue, and her nose would lose sensation. At these times, I didn't know what was coming next; I was devastated! Through so many examples of divine intervention, I had thought that a miraculous cure would soon be forthcoming. Now I was faced with an obvious and serious reversal.

Our Spiritual Father was most generous with his time. On days that we did not see him, we would telephone. It was commonplace for him to bless us over the phone. We had an efficient communication system most of the time, but on many occasions when I called him, the system became incredibly poor. What persistent difficulty I encountered! During one of these conversations I told him I would pray for him to receive the same gift which many years before had been granted to Saint Anthony Mary Claret. The gift about which I spoke was the miraculous retention within himself of the Holy Eucharist. Father then responded in these words: "Francis, I already have it." In a subsequent conversation, I told him that this revelation gave me unparalleled inner peace which lasted for an entire day. I was deeply grateful and awe struck with such a disclosure. He said that this sacred privilege was given to him in Chicago, on Holy Thursday, in 1941. I now learned that he resembled St. Anthony

Claret not only in prayer, but also in this indescribable grace. Never, when praying with us, did he exclude St. Anthony whose virtues he extolled.

Father also spoke to me of his earlier years in Chicago, where he knew a holy woman, a nun, I believe, who had the power to heal. She told him that one day he too would be given this power. On Holy Thursday, a community of sisters, perhaps including this nun, had been in the chapel with Father when he received the Eucharistic privilege. They had seen rays emanating from the tabernacle toward him as he received the gift of retention of the Sacred Species. This wonderful grace delighted me so much that I wanted to tell everybody about it. Father would not allow that, however. When I asked for permission to speak of this marvelous gift, in profound humility he would deny me. Finally, one day, I was able to get his approval to tell certain persons. After that, he reluctantly conceded to me in this matter. When in his company, the Divine

Presence was most often sensed.

Father's keen insight into the lives of certain individuals was unusual. On one occasion, early in our acquaintance, I made a general confession during which he proceeded to speak for me, stating the necessary details which I had difficulty in supplying. He then asked if he had been correct. I assured him that he had.

On a smoggy day, while driving to Los Angeles, I had a problem with one of my eyes. I had already seen a doctor about it and applied the medicine, but smog brought about greater irritation. I really didn't think it looked as bad as it felt. I was surprised, during his discourse, when Father called attention to my pain and volunteered his blessing. The doctor had told me that this chalazion could be treated, but it was chronic. However, after his blessing, Father said that my eye would be well. And so it was. I no longer needed the medicine.

It was also possible for Father to detect

cancer by smell. He told me of this capability on a few occasions.

Whenever we would talk of the sicknesses and calamities which occur in life, Father was consistent and emphatic in his explanation that God <u>permits</u> these things to happen. When, perhaps, I might say in my discussion that God allows things to happen, Father would be quick to correct me, saying: "God permits it to happen." This word "permits" was very important to Father Aloysius.

It is consoling to recall Father's description of the role of the deceased. He said that our dear departed ones are separated from us as though by a veil. We should never think that we are forgotten or alone for they are closer to us in death than they were in life. How comforting this fact can be when we feel that we have lost someone forever.

On First Friday, whenever Marion could muster the strength, we would both attend Father's Mass.

On June 2, 1961, First Friday, Marion was

feeling particularly depressed. She used her last bit of energy to make the trip. Pretty soon, I realized that it would be a major problem for her to get to the altar at Communion time. Since I was serving the Mass, I was not readily available to assist her. This problem concerned me. I pondered how many other people attending this Mass were also seriously ill. Father was always surrounded by sick people. Once again, God used Father Aloysius to display His concern in our turmoil. At Communion time, without any hesitation, Father strode off the altar and worked his way through the crowd. He went directly to Marion and gave her Holy Communion.

The lives of Marion and Father were closely linked. During the early part of 1961, Marion grew progressively worse until about summertime. Needless to say, Father was praying incessantly for her. Then, strangely, Father became sick himself, and he gradually grew worse. Simultaneously, Marion gradually grew better. This situation continued until she had gone from death's door to apparently complete health. She was able to drive her car and function in her household, just as before. At this time, Father, however, was dying; x-rays showed a tumor in his head. Later, on many occasions he recounted this era of his life. He prayed to Our Blessed Mother that she would heal him and allow him therefore to continue helping people. As usual, he re-dedicated himself to her. He related that the Blessed Mother then placed her hand on his head, and he was instantly cured. Moments later, when they were preparing for surgery, the doctor looked at the latest x-rays of Father's head. When he saw that Father had been miraculously cured, he prostrated himself on the floor.

Now, both Father and Marion were well again. This respite, however, was short lived. On the day before the feast of the Immaculate Conception in December 1961, while at the Claretian House, Marion and I went into the garden. She sensed a recurrence of her malady. From then onward, her health faded.

She spent most of the time in bed; she suffered acutely. Her headaches were torturous and the accompanying nausea was most discomforting. She now had cerebral metastasis. On the Feast of Our Lady of Lourdes, February 11, 1962, she fell into a coma and died early the next morning, exactly one year after we had become daily communicants. On each of the days prior to her death, I had been phoning Father. During these conversations, invariably, I reflected on how many days were remaining to complete one year of daily Communions. In effect, I was unknowingly giving a countdown to her death. Her painful journey had ended. I phoned Father Aloysius at 4:00 A.M. and again received his solace. He thought that Marion had gone straight to Heaven, but he would say Mass for her at 6:30 A.M. Thus, by virtue of the "heroic privilege" that he had, her soul would be released to Heaven, if it had gone to Purgatory. She died wearing her brown Scapular after giving a gallant example of conformance to God's Will and bearing the suffering which it entailed. Marion's spiritual state, molded by Father, can best be expressed by her own words on the last Christmas card she gave to me:

"Our Prayer--God's Will be done.
Holy Mother help us!"

DIVINE CONSOLATION

On Tuesday, February 13th, Father Aloysius came to our church, Holy Name of Mary, with Fr. Frank Ambrosi, C.M.F., and two Claretian Brothers to recite the Rosary. On February 14th, Father conducted the funeral and said Requiem High Mass with Fr. Ambrosi and a Fr. Barron, also a Claretian. Father Ambrosi delivered the eulogy. Later, Father Aloysius told me that he, himself, wanted to speak but hesitated for fear that the people would think his homily was strange. He proceeded to give his sermon to me in private. Father said Marion's suffering was like the Sorrowful Mysteries of the Rosary. Her mental anguish upon learning of her disease was analogous to the first mystery, the Agony in the Garden. The second, her severe back aches were like the Scourging. The third, her excruciating headaches resembled the Crowning with Thorns. The fourth, she Carried her Cross. The fifth mystery was her Death.

Father was our very dear friend. Not only was he supportive during this arduous trial, but he remained my Spiritual Father thereafter.

On certain occasions after Marion's death, I began to feel the overwhelming power of God in a manner most difficult to describe--totally peaceful, totally encompassed, a sense of utmost satisfaction. Upon the first occurrence of these events, I immediately sought out Father for an explanation. He was very happy for me and said that what I had was the "experiential presence" of God. I was humbled beyond words.

We often talked about these experiences because Father would query me about their frequency. I remember telling him that there never was any way to predict such an event; it could be while I was at Mass or even when I was completely engrossed in some non-spiritual endeavor. His prayers and intercessions to Our Lady were the means by which I obtained many graces.

Also in 1962, shortly after Marion's death, a priest at St. Joseph's Church in Pomona,

Father Jerome Cummings, made a very strange statement to me in the confessional. Here was a priest that I had never met, telling me something that was seemingly impossible. As usual, I raced to Father Aloysius and told him what the priest had said. I knew that it would require an instant miracle for the priest's strange prediction to be correct. When hearing of this incident, Father Aloysius was greatly pleased and told me that he had prayed that I would receive this grace. Through his prayers I did immediately receive a miracle from God as the priest in the confessional had foretold.

Since I had six young children to raise, the oldest being twelve and the youngest two, I wanted to take special care of my health for their sake. During a routine physical examination, the doctor reported that I had ischemia of the left ventricle in my heart. Perhaps this was true, perhaps they had made an error. In any event, after receiving Father's blessing and returning to the doctor, a new electrocardiogram showed no problem whatsoever.

I recall one particular First Friday when we were having the usual guild meeting and breakfast in the garden. Father introduced me to a prominent screen actress and her family. It was a joyful reunion as they gathered around him in gratitude. The mother had just been released from the hospital, perfectly well. Father had blessed her and prayed that she be cured from terminal cancer when she had but a few days to live. During the second Joyful mystery, she was cured -- Father always had a special love for the Visitation. When this woman died about three months later, Father's explanation to my "why" was that God apparently wanted to give her more time.

During the year 1954, while in New Orleans before we moved to California, I had experienced a spontaneous pneumothorax, a sudden lung collapse. It was weeks before I was able to return to work and months before I felt right again. Thus, in these later years while in California when I experienced the same pain, I likened it to my previous ailment. I phoned Father and received his blessing. Again I was well. Of course, without a medical diagnosis, it is not certain that this "attack" was identical to the former condition, but whatever it was, it was gone.

A friend of Father's, Sister Lucy, was to make her profession in the Carmelite Order in Long Beach on April 27, 1962. I was privileged to drive Father there and witness the celebration. This event gave him great satisfaction as did all sacred ceremonies. I too was profoundly edified and thankful to have been asked to accompany him. It was on such trips as this, when Father and I were alone and didn't have the interruption of door bells and telephones that I profited from his counseling.

It was Father's delight to visit the Los Angeles County Fair in Pomona whenever possible. At times I felt guilty offering Father such a trip when he appeared too tired; yet, I knew that he wanted me to do so. I would drive him there, and he would particularly enjoy the flower and garden displays. He continually found new strength in his admiration for God's creation. At times like this, his energy far exceeded mine.

One Sunday afternoon in 1962, while attending the novena at the Provincial House, I saw a friend of mine, Bob Mihalco. Until this time I had not realized that he was a Catholic. After the novena, he and his wife, Rolande, received Fr. Aloysius' blessing because she had melanoma. It was not long after this meeting that we became good friends, and I visited the Mihalcos frequently. In their effort to gain a further understanding of their faith, they posed many questions to me. I was happy to aid them in any way possible, and though I answered their inquiries, I felt fearful that I might not be answering their questions well enough and unknowingly lead them into error. I doubted my capability and was fearful of the responsibility of guiding these concerned souls at a time of such great distress. I expressed my uneasiness to Fr. Aloysius, and he responded: "Go visit them as often as possible, and don't worry about your answers to their questions. I will send my Guardian Angel with you." Thereafter, regardless of the difficulties in my schedule, I found time to drive from La Verne to Ontario frequently. Many times I took my son, Dan, with me so that he could visit with Bob's young son, Kurt. Thankful to have the assistance of Father's Guardian Angel, I proceeded to accept and answer all inquiries, and we had many pleasant spiritual visits. Bob and I would even see each other sometimes during the day, since we both worked at the same company. I would often repeat to him the worn out phrase: "Let me know if there is something that I can do for you." We wonder if such a statement will ever elicit a response. In this case, the day came that brought a response. On September 6, 1962, Bob called me to say that Rolande was dying, and could I please bring Fr. Aloysius to her. Surely I couldn't promise to do so, because I didn't know Father's availability, but I told Bob that I would do my best. Then, by a brief phone call

I was quickly assured that he would be glad to visit Rolande, but he had no transportation. Fortunately I was able to get off of work. I picked up Father, and we began our fifty mile drive to Ontario. Aside from Father's greeting to me, he hardly said another word; but we prayed, and we prayed. Before the day was over, Father had recited thirty-five decades of the Rosary during our travels.

When we arrived at the Mihalco residence, Bob took us to Rolande, who lay in bed with a gaunt expression on her face. It was obvious that she was in a coma. Father prayed over her and blessed her, but she remained motionless, her mouth open, and her eyes in a blank stare. Father then decided to give Rolande a special blessing for the dying, so that she might receive a plenary indulgence. During this blessing, she briefly changed her expression, apparently indicating acknowledgement of the indulgence. She then lapsed back into her previous state. After many prayers and words of comfort to Bob and to Rolande's sister, a nurse, who was there caring for her, Father left. While riding back to Los Angeles, he continued his prayers as before -- reverently, tirelessly and hopefully. Then I dropped Father off and proceeded back to my home in La Verne. When I arrived, I was told that Bob had phoned, and I should call him back immediately, which I did. He said that Rolande had died. I went to his house at once. Now, even though she was dead, Rolande appeared exactly as she had before: mouth open, gaunt face and blank stare. We knelt at the foot of her bed and again prayed the Holy Rosary. Then, leaving Rolande's sister, Alice, in the room, Bob and I went into the living room to await the undertaker who had already been called. While we sat there, Alice came in at least three times, urging us to come back into the bedroom to see Rolande. Each time we excitedly went with her, and each time we witnessed a progressive change in Rolande's countenance. Her mouth and eyes were closing, and her face was now becoming relaxed.

Finally, when the time came to remove her body, I vividly recall sitting with Bob as she was rolled through the living room. There was a beautiful, peaceful smile on her face. It was obvious that Father's prayers had been heard.

During his lifetime, the sanctity of Father Aloysius shone forth like a beacon. Many people searched him out; they constantly sought his blessing, his prayers and his advice. After his novena services, it was commonplace to see a table laden with religious articles awaiting his blessing. Father responded to this devotion with a total giving of himself. He met their needs with tender compassion. His paternal concern for the poor and the bereaved exemplified Christ Himself.

Father displayed an affection for many of the saints. His particular devotion for Saint Therese, The Little Flower, was evident when he gave me some beautiful rose petals which were in an envelope inscribed: "Roses blessed with the Carmelite Blessing of Saint Therese on her feast day, October 3, 1962, by Father

Aloysius, C.M.F., who has the necessary special faculties granted by the Carmelite Provincial of the United States."

Father gave me several books. In each of these he wrote a few words of encouragement. Particularly, I recall the "Little Office of The Blessed Virgin Mary," published by the Newman Press, and "The Sanctifier," by Archbishop Martinez. An important work that Father recommended was: "The City of God," by Sister Mary of Agreda, published by the Ave Maria Institute. He had read the four volumes written by this holy nun and firmly advocated this private revelation. Father George J. Blatter, under the pen name of Fiscar Marison, provided this superb translation from the original authorized Spanish edition. In fact, Fr. Blatter himself, had given Father Aloysius a copy of his work many years ago. Because of the strong influence which Father's recommendations carried with me, I borrowed "The City of God" from Katherine Morrow and eagerly read all volumes. After completing the series,

I was especially impressed by the section within volume four, the Coronation, (page 297 to page 331) which deals with the experiences of St. James during his apostolate to Spain. The difficulties which this saint encountered prompted him to beseech the aid of Our Blessed Lady who was still alive. In response to his prayers, she was transported by the Angels to Granada where he was imprisoned. She also went to him in Saragossa. There she left her own likeness, carved by the Angels, placed atop a marble or jasper column, which at her command was to be housed within a church to be built in her name. She promised that abundant graces from Almighty God would be granted here through her intercession, provided that we ask in sincere piety and with true faith. At once, Saragossa rose to special significance in my life. I longed for the day when I could visit there to pray for the signal intercession of Our Holy Mother.

In early 1963, Father was sent to Spain; it was a sad day indeed when he left. Before going, he gave me a delightfully sweet statue of St. Joseph with the Child Jesus at about eight years of age, standing on His toes, reaching up to His father. St. Joseph, in turn, is bent at the waist, so that he can cup the Child's head in his hands. This statue is my most prized possession.

Father was gone now, and I had lost my source of guidance. Once, however, when I felt that I needed his help, I did not hesitate to telephone him in Bilbao. He and I had previously discussed the situation at issue, and he had told me that when he went to Saragossa, he would ask the Blessed Mother my question. Due to the great difference in time, my telephone connection with Father was not completed until about one o'clock in the morning, California time. I was elated to hear Father's voice; until now, our only communication had been by mail. He explained to me why my call had been completed at that precise time. He had just returned from Saragossa and felt that he had an answer to my prayer.

Eagerly I listened, for Father's voice was coming through very well. Then, all of a sudden, when he began to tell me what the Blessed Mother had said, I could no longer understand him, for his voice was drowned out by a violent rattling of the doorknob in my bedroom. After several seconds, the rattling ceased, but Father had finished giving his message. I told him that I couldn't understand what he said and asked him to repeat it. Graciously, he did so, but again I was victimized by the rattling of my doorknob. How could this be? I knew my children were asleep. After waiting for the noise to stop, I asked Father again to repeat his message. He said that the devil didn't want me to hear it; so he repeated it again, and this time his words were quite discernible. By a subsequent search of the house, I ascertained that all of the children were, in fact, asleep.

On July 27, 1963, when in Bilbao, Father wrote a most touching letter:

"--------If God wants me to be isolated from

my friends in America, may His Holy Will be most welcome. It is a great consolation for me to pray for your intentions, but particularly for your own self, dear Francis. May I beg of you most humbly to pray that I be always identified with the Holy Will of God without counting the cost. You are a tremendous friend to me and I need your prayer and your sacrifice in the future as much or more than in the past. I will pay you back with all that I am and with all that I have before the throne of the Almighty God.

Most gratefully in the I. Heart of Mary
Fr. Aloysius Ellacuria
C.M.F.

After these events, I longed more than ever to go to Saragossa. Some years later, when Father had returned to the states, and he was arranging to lead a pilgrimage to European shrines, including Saragossa, I prayed to be able to go with him. Such a trip, however, was impossible, because my children were too young for me to leave them. Many people accompanied Father, including Katherine Morrow and Mary Naughten. Several months later, I met Mary through Katherine Morrow and the prayers of Fr. Aloysius.

Later in 1963, Father returned from Spain. When he was in Phoenix, I took my family there several times to see him. We went by automobile, bus and plane: whatever was necessary at the time. On the first visit, he was in the hospital, and when I went to his room, he reached down and pulled out a relic of St. Anthony Claret to give me. Did he know that I had prayed for this?

We also visited Father when he was the pastor at Immaculate Heart Of Mary Church in Phoenix. His mind was occupied with the events surrounding a wedding that he had performed just a few days earlier. He had prayed ardently for the young couple during the ceremony and long after it. Father recalled how the new bride had selected a single white rose to be dedicated to the Blessed Mother.

It was placed beneath the picture of Our Lady which adorned the wall just above the votive candles. It was summertime now in Phoenix, about three days later. The temperature was 109 degrees, and right above the candles where the rose was situated it must have been 130 degrees or so. Yet, this rose was fresh as ever: it had not lost any of its texture. When I walked with Father through the church, we paused with a smile as we looked up at the rose. It was certainly unusual for a rose to behave this way, but I had become accustomed to the unusual. The next day when I was preparing to leave Phoenix, Father shared with me his new found data. Upon close examination he found out that the beautiful white rose was a beautiful white artificial rose. For sure, Father was only human.

Surely, San Antonio wasn't too far to drive either; so we went to see Father when he was there also. Wherever Father was stationed, he reflected in his actions the piety and humility that were his hallmark. All assignments were accepted with holy obedience.

Even muscles bruised in Little League baseball responded to Father's plea. I remember our son, Steve, confidently placing his sore leg in Father's care. A much more serious leg ailment also was cured when Steve Damico met Father and sought relief for his long standing feverish illness. Cellulitis infection in his leg would produce a 105 degree temperature. Subsequently, although he sustains minor inconvenience, he has no major problem with his leg. He is able to participate in sporting events, and the fever no longer exists.

When Mary Naughten and I were contemplating marriage in 1969, we visited Father Aloysius. While driving to Los Angeles for this visit, we began discussing a certain scriptural passage. It was not a lengthy discussion, for it took only a few minutes. Upon our arrival, Father greeted us cordially and counseled us for a half hour or so. Then he blessed us, and we prepared to leave. We had gone out the front door, closed it and were walking away, when Father opened the door just slightly, enough to put his head through, and made a few comments on the identical biblical passage that Mary and I had previously discussed in private. Without a further word, but with a big smile, Father closed the door again and disappeared. In our talk Father had advised us to get married. Surely with his final message on departure, we were convinced that we should do so.

In Mary, I had been blessed with a helpmate to raise the children. She had known Father Aloysius independently and had grown spiritually through attendance at his devotions.

After our marriage, we soon moved to Alta Loma where Father visited us many times. He was able to relax and take siestas in our peaceful environs.

Sister Mary Joseph Bialgues, a member of the Order called: "The Little Sisters of Christ The King," came to the United States from France in January 1970, through the courtesy of Rita and Mary Ellen Benziger. Father Aloysius was informed of her forthcoming visit, and on December 6, 1969, in preparation for this event, he solicited the aid of Charles Carpenter as an interpreter. This holy nun had an extraordinary gift of grace, the gift of counsel. On many occasions she used this gift for the benefit of those who sought her guidance. It seemed perfectly natural that Father Aloysius should be involved with a nun who was so gifted. At Father's invitation, Mary and I met Sister Bialgues at the Benziger home. It was a fruitful spiritual experience to spend an afternoon with these two gifted mystics.

Sister Bialgues remained in this country about five weeks before returning to France early in February of 1970. on March 8, 1976, she died in her native country.

Sister had come from a very large family, and during the Second World War, she, along with her brothers and sisters did whatever they could to aid the French Resistance. One of her brothers was frequently subjected to search by the Germans, and her family often was in hiding. At one time, Sister herself was taken prisoner by the Germans to a tower in Amiens. She was placed in a dungeon within the tower. Deprivation from food and drink in these confines had exacted a severe toll on her health. Yet, in spite of this handicap, she was to continue her life of devoted service for many years to come and provide spiritual sustenance to those who needed her.

In 1976, Father led another pilgrimage to Europe, and again he would include Saragossa in the itinerary. I hoped to make this trip and prepared by getting my passport. As the time grew closer, I felt once more that I should remain at home with my family. Here went my last opportunity to visit Saragossa with Father Aloysius. How many times had I prayed that I would make such a trip.

In October of 1979, my time arrived to make a pilgrimage to Europe! In order to make certain that I wouldn't miss Saragossa, I scheduled that shrine to be the first of our stops. Thus, on the feast of the Holy Rosary, my wife, Mary, and I departed for Spain. The day that we arrived in Saragossa, I was 54 years, 3 months and 28 days old. Remarkably, my age had almost coincided with the age of Our Lady when she had visited St. James in Saragossa. The City of God (page 331 of the Coronation) states that she was 54 years, 3 months and 24 days old at that time.

The faithful from all stations in life were ministered to by Father Aloysius. He gave his time wherever it was needed. No sickness was hopeless, nor was any ailment too minor to gain heartfelt concern. An illustration of this concern was displayed for our daughter, Ann. It was after dark on a rainy Christmas night, in 1977, that he came up our driveway for what was to be his last visit to our home. Ann had gone to see him a couple of months earlier, and he wanted to remind her that he was praying for her intentions.

Father was always eager to see whoever needed him. Ben, my neighbor, was a case in point. I didn't know he was my neighbor until he got sick. When his absence in the community became apparent, it was brought to my attention. I visited Ben, learned that he was critically ill and was a fallen away Catholic. Thinking that perhaps he would like to return to his faith, I broached the subject. It didn't take long to find out that Ben didn't even want to talk about his faith.

Our visits were friendly as long as our discussions were limited to National Geographic, Reader's Digest, outdoor life and nature in general. Although he was confined to bed, his mind roamed through God's creation.

At one time, he was agreeable to a brief visit by our local priest and at a later date accepted a short visit by Father Aloysius. Even now, Ben still wasn't ready.

Father prayed for him during the following weeks. Along with the many other intentions that were constantly put forth to him, he now had Ben in his daily prayers. Soon Ben went to the hospital and soon too, he became agreeable to prayer. On succeeding days, with each recital of the Hail Mary, he grew more peaceful. Now through Father's prayerful intercession, Ben was able to turn to God. It was no longer difficult for him to accept his faith and put it into practice. Ben then died in peace.

Mary and I continued to attend the Third Saturday Guild Mass and avail ourselves of the opportunity of seeing Father. When he became too ill to come to our home, we were most fortunate to be able to continue visiting with him at various locations. We made frequent trips to the Hollywood Presbyterian Medical Center where at one time he was convalescing. We also saw him at the St. John of God Nursing Home in Los Angeles and made one trip to the Carmel Residence at Fallbrook where the Carmelite Sisters cared for him. Our last hospital visit was a very brief meeting with Father at St. John's in Santa Monica.

Father's illnesses now became more frequent and of longer duration.

ETERNAL REWARD

Early in 1981, Father's recurring heart problem brought about a steadily diminishing physical capability. It was consoling to know that Kevin Manion, a very dear friend of his, was ever present to help him.

In March, I took Mary and her father, Malachy Naughten, to the Claretian House. When we saw Father, he had just left the chapel and was walking with difficulty down the hallway. He immediately reached out and blessed us. He expressed his compassion to Malachy who had recently lost his dear wife, Mary.

On April 6, 1981, Father Aloysius died. Mass of the Resurrection was concelebrated on Thursday April 9, at 7:30 P.M. at the San Gabriel Mission. Bishop Juan Arzube was the principal celebrant -- fondly, Father had cradled the Bishop's head in his arms when we gathered to celebrate Father's 50th Anniversary to the priesthood in 1979. Now, before beginning the Holy Sacrifice, Bishop Arzube stopped in procession before the altar and announced that Father had been close to us in life, and he remains close in death. "He has already answered my question," the Bishop said. He had asked what it was like to be in Heaven. Father told him that whatever we have to endure here on earth amounts to nothing in comparison to the treasure that God has in store for us. With that, the Bishop continued up the steps and began Mass. The church was full. I estimated 1300 people to be in attendance. I was later told that there were approximately 300 additional people outside who could not fit into the church. Father William King, the Claretian Superior, who had been so kind through the years, allowing me to see Father Aloysius frequently, had invited me to serve as a pallbearer.

On Friday, April 10th, after the 10:00 A.M. Rosary, Father was buried as he has wished, in the San Gabriel Mission grounds, where he had walked with me and where I now helped to bear his body.

No single individual impacted my life as did Father Aloysius. His spiritual guidance will remain with me forever. Even after his death, I am not abandoned. In July 1976, I began to experience a new series of physical setbacks. For five years I underwent every test that the doctors prescribed -- all to no avail. My prayers seemed to provide no relief. Then, in 1981, my illness left me completely when Father Aloysius went to his eternal reward.

Now we all have a powerful intercessor who stands in Perpetual Adoration before the throne of God. He will remember each of us and will look with particular fatherly care upon the fledglings of his own formation: MISIONEROS DE ADORACION PERPETUA.

In Fatima, Portugal, on February 9, 1972, Father Aloysius founded the Missionaries of Perpetual Adoration of the Most Blessed Sacrament and Perpetual Veneration of the Immaculate Heart of Mary. This group strives to emulate the heroic life of its founder and put into their daily practice his constant diligence to prayer.

PERSONAL DATA

Fr. John Aloysius Ellacuria Echevarria, CMF

Born on June 21, 1905, in the town of Yurre, Province of Vizcaya, Spain.

Father and Mother were Raymond and Martha.

Baptized on June 22, 1905, in Yurre in the parish of Our Lady of the Assumption by Fr. Mariano Echevarria.

First Holy Communion was on February 2, 1912, at Our Lady of the Assumption from the hands of the pastor, Fr. Hilario de Soloeta.

Confirmed in 1913 in Assumption parish by Bishop Cadena y Eleta, Titular of Vitoria, Alba, Spain.

Family home was in a suburb of Yurre called Caserio-Orue Barrio de San Cristobal, Yurre, Vizcaya, Spain. Raymond Ellacuria's occupation was that of a proprietor of farms, mountains and pastures and woody groves in and around Yurre.

Entered the Congregation on July 29, 1916, in the minor Seminary in Valmaseda, Vizcaya, Spain under the Perfect John Anthony Uriarte and Superior Jose Calvo.

Reception of the Holy Habit of the Congregation was on August 14, 1920, from the hands of Most Rev. Father Martin Alsina, CMF, Superior General.

Priestly Ordination was on November 3, 1929, in the city of Burgos by the Archbishop Dr. Emmanuel De Castro.

> Hail Immaculate Heart
> of Mary —
>
> My dearest friend Francis Levy
> May the Immaculate Heart
> of Mary keep you always
> within her Heart.
>
> Fr. Alojzius E. Macurra
> C.M.F.
> August 22, 1962

Father's wishes, expressed in his gift of "The Little Office Of The Blessed Virgin Mary".

Father Aloysius with Francis Levy

A postcard from Father Thomas Matin, C.M.F.

Konnersreuth
1 JAN 1961

Reverend and dear Father,

Many greetings from this blessed place are sent to your Reverence

by,

Your most devoted and faithful servant,

Rev. Thomas Matin CMF

(POSTMARKED 8 FEB 1961)

Message on Father Matin's card.

Father Aloysius and Father Ambrosi

Brother Salvatore Azzarello, C.M.F.

Father Aloysius with his Mother and his Brother, Father Jose

At His Desk In Phoenix

Father Aloysius

All my gratitude and prayers for you, my dearest Spiritual Son Francis Xavier Levy and to your children Francis Jr, Linda, Tina, Paul, Dan & Ann. May your Christmas be the very best and your New Year laden with every grace and blessing.

That we may be made partakers of His divinity who has deigned to become partaker of our humanity, Jesus Christ.
(Offertory Prayer of Mass)

Father's Christmas greeting.

Misioneros,
Hijos del Corazón de María
San Francisco, 16

TELÉFONOS 24 58 98 / 22 41 81

✝
Hail Heart of Mary

Bilbao, April 24, 1963

Mrs Frances Leary

My dear Frances,

Many thanks for all your prayers and sacrifices for me. Do continue them because I need all the spiritual help you have been giving me. Likewise the thanks finally did arrive, 8 of them.

Do tell Sister Frances that I am remembering her intentions. Do thank Sister for her check for $25.00

Give my best regards to all your family and friends.

Ever gratefully yours in the Hhof Mary
Fr Florencio F Maceira. C.M.F.

Ever humble.

SEMINÁRIO DO CORAÇÃO DE MARIA
Telef. 97169—FÁTIMA

January 14, 1972

Dear Francis & Mary,

Thank you so much for your most kind letter, and I want you to know that I am most appreciative of your prayers and your concern.
Thank you also for the Mass stipend and offering. It is my privilege to offer Holy Mass each day in this holy place, and here I remember the needs and intentions of all my spiritual children and friends. I have offered the Mass for Louie Greene as you requested, for the repose of his immortal soul.
You may be sure that you are also in my prayers each day, and it is my most earnest prayer that Our Blessed Mother may bestow upon you most abundant grace and blessings in the year ahead. My novices join me in this wish, and in the request that you pray God's continued blessings upon the work that we have begun here in Fátima.

In the Immaculate Heart of Mary,

Fr. Aloysius Ellacuria, C.M.F.

P.S. My best regards to your most lovely children.

Ever prayerful.

MISSIONARIES OF PERPETUAL ADORATION
Apartado 30
FATIMA, PORTUGAL

February 20, 1972

Dear Mr. Levy,

Your kind letter, with generous donation enclosed, have been most gratefully received. Thank you for your special prayers and support for this group that is called: Missionaries of Perpetual Adoration of the Most Blessed Sacrament and Perpetual Veneration of the Immaculate Heart of Mary. These ten young Americans have been so well received here in Fatima by the Bishop and by all the people. Last week the Bishop presented them with a beautiful and historic gift--the first tabernacle that was used in the Basilica of Fatima for seventeen years. It is carved so masterly out of the same kind of oak as of the tree on which Our Blessed Mother appeared in 1917 to the three little shepherds. Today, the 20th of February is the feastday of Jacinta, the day on which she died.

You and your family are in all our prayers, sacrifices, and in my Holy Mass celebrated daily at 12:00 noon. Praying very specially for all your intentions and that Our Lord may accomplish His Will through you, as a wonderful instrument.

May Our Blessed Mother of Fatima grant you very special graces for your spiritual and material welfare.

In the Heart of Our Blessed Mother,

Fr. Aloysius Ellacuria, C.M.F.

Missioneros De Adoracion Perpetua.

MISSIONARIES OF PERPETUAL ADORATION
Apartado 30
FATIMA, PORTUGAL

June 6, 1973

Mr. and Mrs. Francis X. Levy
7124 Hellman Avenue
Alta Loma, California 91701

Dear Mr. and Mrs. Levy:

Thank you for your beautiful letter of May 29th and the generous donation enclosed. Thank you for remembering me. I will save the $55.00 for a trip, as Our Lord may have that in mind for me soon.

God loves your childlike feelings toward Him, and you can be assured that you are loved with predilection by Him and His Blessed Mother. Interior trials serve principally to purify our motives of love of God. God is bring you closer to Him.

I hope that this letter reaches you at your new home, where I hope and pray that you will be very happy and live sanctified lives therein. May Our Lord bless you and your new home and every day that you live and work in it.

Praying always for you and all your intentions.

In the Most Blessed Sacrament
and the Immaculate Heart of Mary,

Fr. Aloysius Ellacuria, C.M.F.

The value of interior trials.

Fr. Aloysius Ellacuria, C.M.F.

CLARETIAN MISSIONARIES
1119 WESTCHESTER PLACE
LOS ANGELES, CALIFORNIA 90019
PHONE: (213) 731-9329

PROVINCIAL HOUSE

July 19, 1974

Mr. Francis Levy
7124 Hellman Avenue
Alta Loma, Calif. 91701

Dear Francis,

This letter comes as a warm greeting to you and your dear family.

I appreciate all your visits, Francis, and always enjoy our conversations very much.

Enclosed you will find the address where you can obtain the books written by Anna Emerick.
Divine Love
P.O. Box 24
Fresno, Calif. 93707

Give my very special regards to Mary and the children and you receive the same. Please be assured of my prayers for all of you.

May God bless you all and keep you always close.

Sincerely yours in the
Immaculate Heart of Mary,

Father Aloysius Ellacuria, CMF

Father was interested in the four volumes of Anna Catharina Emmerick.

Fr. Aloysius And His Brother, Fr. Jose Maria, With Their Sister, Poli, And Her Husband And Children

Father Aloysius Blesses Religious Articles

**CLARETIAN
PRIESTS & BROTHERS**

PROVINCIAL RESIDENCE

March 1981

My Dearest friends,

My sincerest thanksgiving for your Christmas greetings and donation this past holiday season.

My deepest apologies for this delay, but I have been and continue to be seriously ill. Please pray for me.

May the Blessed Mother obtain for you the choicest graces from Her Divine Child during this Lenten season.

In the Immaculate Heart of our Mother Mary

Father Aloysius Ellacuria, C.M.F.

Father Aloysius Ellacuria, C.M.F.

1119 WESTCHESTER PL., LOS ANGELES, CALIFORNIA 90019   (213) 731-9329

Final letter

www.ingramcontent.com/pod-product-compliance
Lightning Source LLC
Chambersburg PA
CBHW071303040426
42444CB00009B/1855